From Warrior

To

Warrior

PATH
of the
WARRIOR

To my wife Ana María, my most beloved Master.

*To each of these animals, children, men
and women that permitted me to
be what I am: an immensely happy man,
white belt in humanness.*

PATH
of the
WARRIOR

Consult the oracle
for everyday guidance
on your life journey

St. Martin's Press ≈ New York

AN EDDISON•SADD EDITION
Edited, designed and produced by
Eddison Sadd Editions Limited
St Chad's House, 148 King's Cross Road
London WC1X 9DH

Phototypeset in Perpetua MT using QuarkXPress on Apple Macintosh
Origination by C. H. Colour Scan SDN BHD, Kuala Lumpur, Malaysia
Printed by South China Printing Co., Hong Kong

Contents

Foreword

This writing gathers the teachings of my venerable Masters throughout all the years in search of my centre and its connection with the rest of the universe. The path I chose is that of the noble martial arts, legacy of my spiritual ancestors. Thanks to this knowledge I have been able to glimpse the powers of the sky and earth which still sleep inside myself. Thanks to them I have known a world parallel to ours which, on occasion, slightly touches our daily life and covers us with amazement. I have learned that things are not always what they appear to be, and I have found the tools to cultivate sensitivity and love for all the sentient beings of the world. It has been a trail in constant evolution, of questions without definitive answers, of a restless heart and of dreams that drive me to keep taking up the sword that attempts to cut the chains of ignorance and enlightens the Sacred Path of the Warrior.

Introduction

During his life, a Warrior passes through different situations, stages and tests. Each section of the book represents one of these and reflects the way that, according to my humble understanding, a Warrior should act. As he travels on his journey, experience his pleasure and pain, his challenges, successes and defeats – things that we all face in life. He shows us how to learn from each of these experiences.

You may choose simply to follow the Warrior on his cyclical journey through life. But you may also choose to use the Warrior's path as a means of bringing to light the answers that live inside you – either in response to a specific question or to give you guidance for the day ahead. If you wish you can write down the numbers 1 to 36 and place them inside a bag, drawing out a number to direct you to a reading, or you may prefer just to open the book on a random page. Whichever way, you will find the reading that something inside you chooses – the reading that is helpful for you at that moment.

May the words brighten the way. May the mind open. May the sun shine. From heart to heart.

1

The Warrior is Born

The snow has melted,
The forest breathes again.
The sun reflects over the pond ...
Once again.

2

The Warrior Awakens

On the horizon, the limit between heaven and earth blurs. On the horizon, it is impossible to discern. Before watching the sunset, I sit on a stable stone.

You have been living in an unreal state. You lack a basis. You are in the air. All this time you have lived thinking that things were in a determinate way. You have acted accordingly and this is right. But on the path to knowledge, the Warrior must penetrate deeper and deeper inside himself and his life. On the path to knowledge, the Warrior must die only to be reborn again, with fresh insight.

It is the time to awake. Suddenly, you have realized how fragile your beliefs were. Those that used to be your pillars are now only faint thoughts. The Almighty has played the old joke of taking away the chair on which you were going to sit every day. You have hurt yourself, you have felt pain, and this is also good. If you had fallen down over something soft, you would not have paid any attention to it. But the truth is that

you have landed on another reality. You are bewildered, your consciousness flustered. You do not understand anything of what has happened. You feel like you have wasted your time until now, and you may even feel shame for what you did before. Retrospectively, you will see yourself as somebody dedicated to futile things.

The pain blinds. Even if you do not understand it, know that what has happened to you is something marvellous. You are no longer the same as you were some moments ago and, if you are wise enough, you will never be. Other things will matter now, you will climb other mountains. You will face other demons, other brothers will walk along with you. Live your new life, look with new eyes. Nevertheless, be prepared to be reborn. Again. Only by doing so will you be able to reach the end of the way.

3

The Warrior Begins the Journey

You have been too long in this place. The air is rarefied. Your life is stagnant, you do not flow. You must, therefore, leave in search of new dawns.

Your setting no longer brings you new things. Leave the superfluous, take with you only what is essential, the minimum possible. Your heart, your spirit and your body are enough.

Put your affairs in order before you go. Close the circles, leave no loose ends. May your departure be natural, just like the migrating cranes in winter. There is no need to escape. Simply leave this place, this situation, behind. Go. You will surely find new fellow travellers.

You may come back some day.

4

The Warrior Shows his Interior

Even if it hurts, live with the truth. This is the path of the Warrior. This is the only path.

The blade of the sword is sharp and cold. The hilt is rounded and warm. Only this way can I fight. Why do you wear an armour? Why do you fear so much? Nothing serious can happen to you now. Open your heart to sun and life so that the world can reflect in you. If you are embittered, open yourself. Light will come smoothly. If you are happy, open yourself. Light will flow smoothly.

Show the interior. Discard the superficial and free yourself. Live with the truth. If someone deserves coldness, let him receive it. And if someone deserves warmth, this is what he must receive. To caress when there is need to caress. To strike when there is need to strike. May no one be in any doubt about what you are, think or feel.

5

The Warrior Seeks for the Brother

The path will take the rest of your life. And more. Why do it alone? It is good to travel accompanied. Seek then for the brother of the way.

With the brother you will be able to journey the path, equal to equal. Whenever he is tired, you will have to keep rowing. When you sleep, he will have to stay alert. When one of you stumbles, the other will be there to help. When one is ill, the other will run to heal.

Little by little the bonds will strengthen and your hearts will rejoice when embracing after each battle. You will share the sacred and the profane, companions in prayers and in drunkenness. Each one with his own story, his love and his needs, submerged into life. But in the middle of the maelstrom you will remember your friend and your heart will feel comforted.

Year after year you will traverse together the Sacred Path of the Warrior. Back to back, one hundred combats will be one hundred victories. And in a distant day at the end of your lives, you will sit side by side, gazing at the sunset in the silent desert.

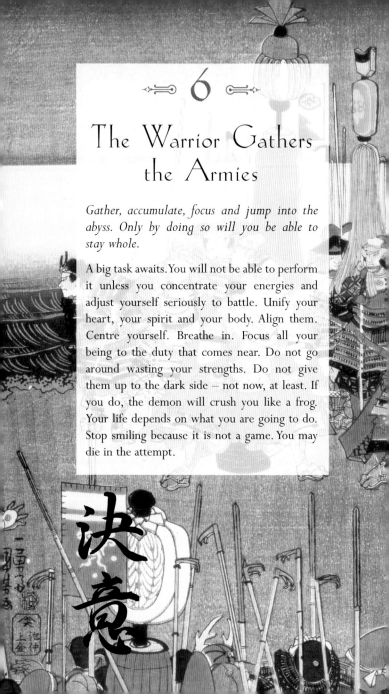

6

The Warrior Gathers the Armies

Gather, accumulate, focus and jump into the abyss. Only by doing so will you be able to stay whole.

A big task awaits. You will not be able to perform it unless you concentrate your energies and adjust yourself seriously to battle. Unify your heart, your spirit and your body. Align them. Centre yourself. Breathe in. Focus all your being to the duty that comes near. Do not go around wasting your strengths. Do not give them up to the dark side – not now, at least. If you do, the demon will crush you like a frog. Your life depends on what you are going to do. Stop smiling because it is not a game. You may die in the attempt.

7

The Warrior Cuts the Chains

You have been a slave of your weakness for a long time. Swing your axe and cut the chains. Only then will you be freed.

You are faced with a big task. You know you have to do it, but you have been postponing it, either because it will be painful or because you feel you are incapable of doing it. But you cannot ignore your inner voice. At some time you will have to take charge of your chariot, so assume your Warrior status and fulfil your duty now. It is a blind act, without possible repentance once started. Do not pay attention to your comfort, nor to your laziness nor your indulgence. Cut the chains and free yourself.

8

The Warrior Searches for the Demon

The demon has harassed you for too long. You have given him a big advantage. If you want to be free you have to exchange roles. Gather your armies before beginning the journey.

It is no longer possible to keep living this way. You are playing his game, he has you at his mercy. Seek the demon inside yourself – dare to look inside. In the journey you may find vermin, but you will also find princesses and masters. They will help you in combat. That does not mean that they will fight for you, but that they may dry the sweat from your brow, wipe the blood from your wounds.

Pursue the demon, harass him, face him. Descend to the bottom of hell in search for him. You will see that he hides himself and avoids your presence. When this happens do not think that you have won the battle. In this moment, do not let cowardliness take possession of you and make you give up the search. If you do not see him

31

when you look for him, look deeper into the unexplored nooks. Hunt him out day and night. Learn to recognize his footprints, the way he smells, his marks. And when you find him, split him open with a single slash of the sword – without anger, but with the strength of the thunder. Observe him carefully. Make sure he is dead. Then ascend back to reality.

You will be triumphant, so stay humble. Seat yourself, breathe. And then continue your way.

9

The Warrior Conceals Himself

The way carries you to a dangerous place. In order to come out unharmed, you must be able to see without being seen.

You must weigh the next step carefully. Conceal yourself, fuse with the ground and keep your eyes wide open. Flex your muscles, gather the armies, contract your body and then release it in a jump. Spring over your enemy. Without noticing it, he will be lost.

⊷⇒ 10 ⇐⊷

The Warrior Stays Alert

A real Warrior stays always guarding, always alert, stalking. You must keep your eyes wide open in order to be able to look inside yourself.

See that your heart is always clean, free and light. Watch the course that your life is taking at this moment. Are you going where you want to go? Or are you simply being dragged? How much of yourself have you given up? In which important things have you made concessions? What is the sense of how you are living now? In what way is this related to your past? What will the consequences be for the future? Are you still keeping the dignity of every Warrior? Is your heart still tender and kind? Is your spirit still so strong that you would jump into the abyss?

One blink is enough, and you will be thousands of miles away from home. Are you happy? A Warrior stays always guarding. A Warrior keeps the eyes always open.

11

The Warrior Shows his Sword

Stand up with dignity over the earth. Show that you are ready to fight until death.

Your hands hold the sword. In profile, its sharp end points forward. Demarcate a territory, be the lord of it. Emanate silent power. All the fury is awakened but concealed, ready to spring forth. May your adversary see that the whole universe is standing in front of him. Roar if it is necessary. Howl like the wolf in the mountains. Bristle your enemy's skin. Intimidate him with a shining glance. The combat will be avoided. Life will be preserved. Retire humbly even when you have triumphed.

This is the way of the Warrior.

通俗水滸傳豪傑百八人之一人

短冥次郎阮小吾

濠州石碣村の産にして胸に
豹の彫物ありて性勇猛みて
能く水中に長く身を潜きと術
を得うり梁山泊の塚軍にして
金沙灘の敵船の大将を捕ふ

一勇齋
國芳画

⚬ 12 ⚬

The Warrior Obstructs the Way

It is enough. You have waited for a long time. You have restrained yourself from acting, waiting for things to take up their natural course once more. But they have not done it. So you must act.

Your enemy has advanced more than he should have. He has trodden over every body and every dignity that he has met on the way. He has left behind many tears and frustrations, and yet he feels no regrets.

You must stop this situation, since you are the strongest one now. So face this person and obstruct the way. If you do not do it, innocent people will keep on suffering from this despot. If your hands are not enough to stop him, use your shield. If your shield is not enough, use your menacing spear. If you still cannot do it, unsheathe your sword and split him in two. Risk losing everything in this combat; if you do, you will always emerge victorious. No matter what happens, you will always emerge victorious.

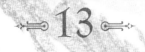

The Warrior Jumps into the Abyss

Jump into the abyss. Risk everything and throw yourself in.

Even if everything around you seems to indicate that you will die, you must take that risk. The hand of the Almighty will save you in the last moment. You will suffer from hunger and cold. You will feel the horror gripping your body as you fall. But do not doubt. If you do so, you will die.

Trust that nothing is going to happen to you. And you will land softly.

14

The Warrior Struggles

The first sunbeams arrive on the beach. The armies have arranged themselves and everything is ready. The battle will break out at any moment. There is no choice. You must struggle.

In doing so, put all your spirit, heart and body into it. Fight centred, unified, aligned. Fight tirelessly, day and night if necessary. Stay alert to the four directions. Trust the animal that lives within. The battle will have peaks and valleys; be sensitive to that and adapt yourself to it.

One time forwards, one time backwards. One time attacking, one time defending. Disperse your adversary, charge him while he is breathing in. Overwhelm him. Do not give him time to gather the armies. Constantly change your strategies. Attack high and then low. Then low and then to the centre. Vary the rhythm of your assaults. One time fast, one time slow. One time slow, one time still.

Be a continuous change from one animal to another, from one element to another. Water against stone. Fire against metal. Wood against

大物浦上月

earth. So, it will be impossible to classify you within a fixed pattern, and therefore you will be unbeatable. Follow your spontaneity and keep yourself light and buoyant. May your adversary not be able to touch you, yet may he feel the power of your blows. Use your hands, your feet, your elbows and your knees. Evade, then counter-attack. Anticipate his movements and neutralize them before they begin. Let him pass and then fall on him. Make his weapons useless.

Shorten the distance, attack and then get out of his reach. Fight with all the energy of your youth.

But more important than all this is to fight without anger. If savagery and cruelty enter your heart, no matter what you do, you will be lost. You will convert yourself into that which you fight, and the dark side will have a new recruit within its lines.

So take firm hold of your sword and enter into battle. After vanquishing, retire in silence. There is nothing to rejoice. Nothing to celebrate. Death is always accompanied by tears. You have only accomplished your duty. Never forget that.

⟞⟞≡ 15 ≡⟞⟞

The Warrior Suffers

Life has put you in a blind alley. You have no way to escape. The only choice left is to suffer.

Do not try to avoid it. On the contrary, seek your pain. Feel it. Dissolve it in your saliva and then swallow it, digest it, assimilate it, make it part of you. Feel the walls of your heart detaching. Feel the muscles ripping away from your bones. Live the disintegration of yourself through your suffering. Consider yourself worthless. A pair of old sandals thrown at the roadside by a tired walker. An empty bottle thrown away by a drunken man without destiny. Consider yourself insignificant, which is what we really are. Cry, blaspheme against your God and burn his image if it is necessary. Listen to the silence of your loneliness. You are alone in the world. No one will be able to do anything for you. You are lost and helpless. Shattered. Once more, disintegrated in adversity. Go down to the depth of your torment. Die in each cell of your body.

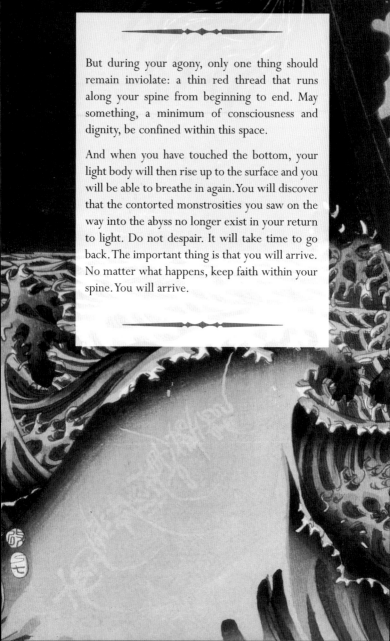

But during your agony, only one thing should remain inviolate: a thin red thread that runs along your spine from beginning to end. May something, a minimum of consciousness and dignity, be confined within this space.

And when you have touched the bottom, your light body will then rise up to the surface and you will be able to breathe in again. You will discover that the contorted monstrosities you saw on the way into the abyss no longer exist in your return to light. Do not despair. It will take time to go back. The important thing is that you will arrive. No matter what happens, keep faith within your spine. You will arrive.

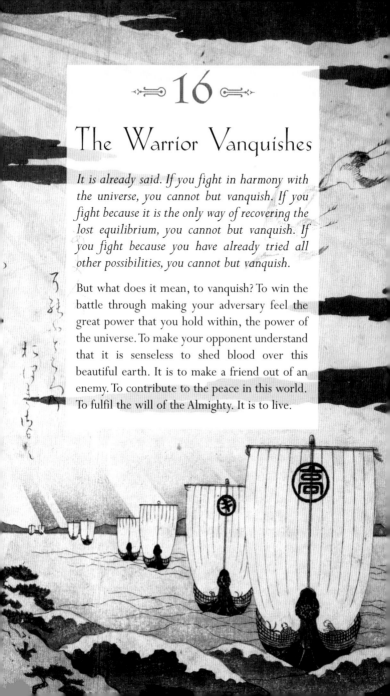

16

The Warrior Vanquishes

It is already said. If you fight in harmony with the universe, you cannot but vanquish. If you fight because it is the only way of recovering the lost equilibrium, you cannot but vanquish. If you fight because you have already tried all other possibilities, you cannot but vanquish.

But what does it mean, to vanquish? To win the battle through making your adversary feel the great power that you hold within, the power of the universe. To make your opponent understand that it is senseless to shed blood over this beautiful earth. It is to make a friend out of an enemy. To contribute to the peace in this world. To fulfil the will of the Almighty. It is to live.

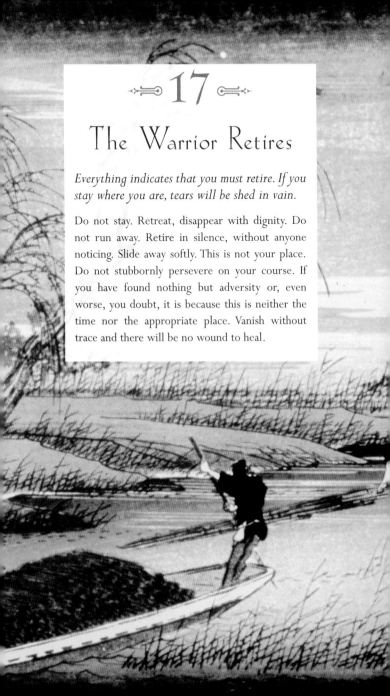

❧ 17 ❧

The Warrior Retires

Everything indicates that you must retire. If you stay where you are, tears will be shed in vain.

Do not stay. Retreat, disappear with dignity. Do not run away. Retire in silence, without anyone noticing. Slide away softly. This is not your place. Do not stubbornly persevere on your course. If you have found nothing but adversity or, even worse, you doubt, it is because this is neither the time nor the appropriate place. Vanish without trace and there will be no wound to heal.

18

The Warrior Hides his Interior

You are very weak now and the struggle grows harder and harder. Close, then, the doors — hide your interior.

Life is precious and does not deserve to be lost to the hands of demons unworthy of taking it. Retire, gather the armies and only then set out in search of the shadows. Not before. Never before.

⟿ 19 ⟿

The Warrior Devotes Entirely

There is only one way to take action: by devoting yourself entirely.

Make a transverse cut across your life and examine it. There are two kinds of things: the useful and the useless. Leave the superfluous and concentrate on the important. Examine the important. Choose now what is really important. It will be evident that you must dedicate yourself to one particular task. In order to do so, gather your armies, take a deep breath and jump. Focus on your goal and never lose sight of it.

Immerse yourself in your task and dedicate yourself to it with Warrior discipline. Work day and night with unbreakable tenacity and will. Rest when it is necessary, repose for a moment and then continue again. But do not neglect your life. You must sleep well and eat healthily to be able to advance.

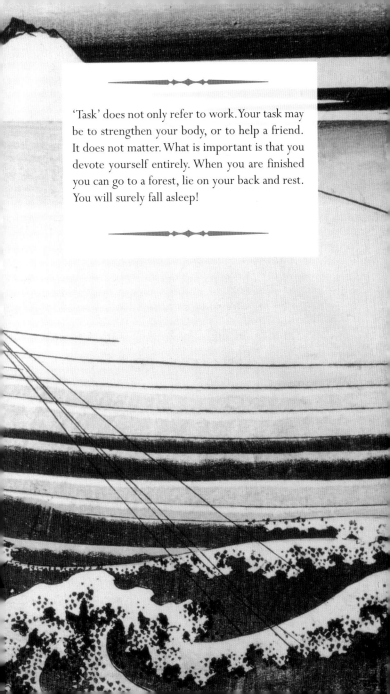

'Task' does not only refer to work. Your task may be to strengthen your body, or to help a friend. It does not matter. What is important is that you devote yourself entirely. When you are finished you can go to a forest, lie on your back and rest. You will surely fall asleep!

愛情

20

The Warrior Loves

May your heart listen to the whisper of the universe, turning slowly around. Open your channels of perception and connect yourself with the Almighty. Join your palms and bow.

It is the time to love. Share the joy of life with those that surround you. Caress the arched back of your cat. Embrace your friend, your brother. Kiss your parents, those who gifted you with life. Make love to your lover. Feel your naked heart, delighted with the rejoicing of freedom that love gives you. Feel it beating, sensitive to life. Free the knots.

21

The Warrior Loses the Path

In the depths of the forest, my hand stretches out trembling. A frog looks at me. Where are you? Not even you know that.

You were on the right track, but something happened on the way and now you are lost. Either you lacked strength or you lacked wisdom. And now you are missing. Will you come back?

Before returning to the source you must ask yourself why it is necessary to do so. Maybe this is where you wanted to arrive and you had not realized it. Or perhaps it may be more convenient to keep walking on and leave your home behind. But if you want to take up the path again, you must first retrace your steps.

Think about it. Where did you want to go? Which mountain were you climbing? You know it, or at least it was once clear to you.

Remember this moment of light and resume the way. You will probably have to return to the origin before you can continue. Do not get lost again. You may not find even a big-eyed friend next time.

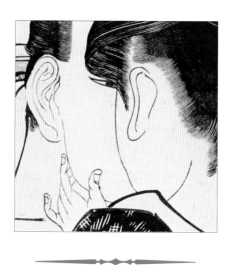

22

The Warrior Enjoys the Wine and his Lover

Once retaining, once releasing. One time containing, one time letting go. This is the time to run riot, to lavish pleasures, not to spare them.

Drink the wine and get drunk in the company of your brother of the way. Feel the whirl of the night that calls you to lose yourself in her thousand dark faces. Walk the streets and return to your bedroom night after night. Enjoy the company of your beautiful and voluptuous lover. Live each orgasm as if it was your last, rejoice your encounters with every inch of your skin. Delight in the scent that emanates from your playmate and coil yourself in her hair. Take pleasure in your nakedness and in the sun bathing your sex. Try each tasty dish that comes your way and savour it because it is unique in the world. Go right to the limit, where you feel the centrifugal force almost pushing you out of this reality.

But during your ecstasy only one thing should remain inviolate: the thin red thread that runs along your spine from beginning to end. May something, a minimum of consciousness and dignity, be confined within this space. This will mean for you the bridge between death and the control of the chariots when you approach the edge of the abyss.

Once retaining, once releasing. One time containing, one time letting go. Afterwards, the time to sit and gather the armies must come. Only so will you be able to stay on the path.

⟿ 23 ⟿

The Warrior is Defeated

To reflect on, to correct, to wait. Then, to act. The sky reflects over the sea and only then looks at the moon.

Once up, once down, one time forwards, one time backwards. This is a moment of defeat for you. You have lost a battle in the way to knowledge. You have lost a combat. Acknowledge it, take charge of your failure. You are responsible for it, you can blame no one else. Either you lacked strength or you lacked wisdom. Essentially, you did not do what you had to do at the appropriate time.

You must accept your mistake with humility. If you caused pain, ask for pardon. If you caused destruction, rebuild. If you caused division, rejoin. The important thing is that you do not commit the same error again. Only this way can the sun shine for you. Now, besides doing all that you can in order to repair what has been damaged, you must be ready to face the consequences that may come from your actions.

24

The Warrior Gazes at the Horizon

Thank the Almighty for all you have lived, all that you are. Connect with your heart, feel it beating. Breathe, listen. Rise and breathe again. Your smile will illuminate the path ...

Leave what you are doing. Seat yourself. Repose. Set your spine upright. Relax your eyes. Gaze at the horizon without focusing on anything in particular. Sweep the infinite with a mild glance. You are part of the universe, son of the sky, of the earth and of time. Brother of the sun and the moon. Your life is related to everything you see. You are part of it. You have all you need to be happy, so do not search further from yourself.

⟡ 25 ⟡

The Warrior Sits

It is the moment to stop acting. Come out from the maelstrom of your life and make a space in which to meditate.

Stay immovable, quieten your spirit. Look for the solitude. Only by doing so will you be able to see clearly. There has been too much movement until now. The horses are runaway, the whirl of your life has turned endlessly around. Set your spine upright, concentrate on the lower abdomen, relax your body, observe your breathing. Close your eyes and make silence. Connect with the earth, feeling the umbilical cord that unites you. Take shelter in your mother's womb. Repose, rest, meditate. Then go and take action if it is required.

↺ 26 ↻

The Warrior Takes Up the Path Again

You are lost. And you have decided to go back to your original path. What to do? First of all, you must not despair. You have not disappeared – you are simply not where you would like to be, that is all. Looked at this way, it is less distressing.

Orient yourself. Where does the sun rise? Where does it set? You now have something clear: your north, at least. Look at the sky. Where is the Celestial Archer? Where the Southern Cross? Reconstruct mentally the way you travelled. At which point exactly did you leave your original path? You are not alone. There are brothers with you. Turn to them for help; they will certainly answer.

If it is night-time, do not move. You do not know what you will find in the forest. You may find guardians, but it is certain that evil spirits will also threaten you. Wait until the sun rises and walk during the day. Ration your food, your

water, your breath and your heartbeats. It may take a while to return your path. If it is winter and all is covered by snow, you have to be even more careful. The landscape is more blurred, the road more difficult to recognize. Take care of the cold, and keep your feet warm in particular. If you have gone too far, you will have to wait until the spring thaws to return. Meanwhile, make an effort to leave marks that other brothers may be able to recognize. If you want help, if you want to be seen, you must stand out. If you are really lost, going into seclusion will not help you.

But most of all do not give up, do not neglect yourself, do not sit down. If you do, the icy mantle of Death will make you hers. If you really want to return, look for a river. Sooner or later you will arrive at the warm sands of the sea.

27

The Warrior Returns to the Origin

You have gone too far. You have lost your roots. You do not remember your father or your mother, nor your land. These territories are too unfamiliar for you, maybe dangerous. You are a foreigner.

You are no longer the person you were, not even the person you always wanted to be. What is the sense in staying? Do not persist in this direction. More and more, the wind will restrain your march. Do not keep on moving forward. If you continue to do so, you may never be able to return home. You will lose the way for ever and wander errant through strange lands.

So return to your origin, to your roots. Go up the river and take shelter in the womb. You will feel protected as a child again. You will be what you were before you became lost. You will feel your mother's love, the security of her warmth. No one will be able to hurt you there. You are safe. You will have to recover before beginning a

new journey. You are too weak now, although you are unaware that this is the case. Be patient, renew your energies. You will soon feel secure, ready to undertake your journey once more. Before you depart, kiss your mother, your father and your land.

28

The Warrior Reaffirms the Bonds

To cut the chains and to reaffirm the bonds. This is. To eliminate the useless and to put down roots from which to grow. This is.

In your life you have, little by little, moved away from the important, from what is – for you – important. And this is no good. May you never be so busy so as to let this happen. If so, you will roam erratically through unknown worlds.

Visit your beloved parents. They are old and in need of you. Embrace them, kiss them, express to them all the love you have. May there not be any doubt left in their minds that they are of the utmost importance to you. You can return to your birth place, to your childhood house. To look for those with whom you used to play. To ask your mother to make your favourite dessert that you used to eat eagerly when you were seven years old. Or to look for your Warrior ancestors, to visit their graves, to take something of yours as a tribute. To reread their

writings, to burn a stick of incense for them or to sit and meditate close to them.

Retrace your steps and return to your roots. Revere your beloved Master. Look also for your brother. Hug him as you did one hundred years ago, after a big battle. Go back home in body and spirit. Wait for your mate, who will soon come ready to enfold you in her arms. Perhaps caress her tenderly, looking into her eyes just as you did when you walked together for the first time.

Retrace your steps and return to your roots. Return to yourself. Return to life. It is already time.

尊敬

29

The Warrior Honours his Master

The Master has been waiting for you for a long time. You have left his side and abandoned him. The Master must always be respected, honoured, so retrace your steps and return to your roots.

Foolish disciple. Have you forgotten the old noble traditions? Your Master has made a powerful Warrior of you. He welcomed you as a son when you went back to him. He has healed your wounds, and listened patiently to your unending questions. He has always had time for you. Go back, return to your roots.

Honour your beloved Master.

30

The Warrior Clears the Way

The decision lies in your hands. You can let it pass or you can restrain it. To open the way or to close it.

You are doubtful because you do not know what the consequences will be. Nevertheless, what is to be done now is to clear the way for your disciple. Help him to continue on the path, free from obstacles. It is written in the stars that he must reach the summit of this mountain. But he is neither strong nor wise enough for gathering the armies and drawing the bow. So fight in front of him, protecting him, until the battle is won. Then, at dawn, when your disciple rests, retire yourself in silence without leaving a trace.

常磐御前

九條院の雜仕宇多部の女
左馬頭義朝の妾となり今若
乙若牛若の三子を產り平治の
乱に義朝野間の内海にて
亡ぶ後伏見の里小さき
いぶ隱るを美人とて
清盛是を愛すめ
うぶ婦の
道を教へて三人の子を失はず
再び源家を起こし平家を亡ぼしなり

31

The Warrior Protects

Someone needs help. He is in danger and does not know how to face it, perhaps does not even know the risk he is running. It is your duty to take part in the battle.

You cannot pretend you are not aware of it. He will not be able to do it by himself. He's too young, too weak, so it is your responsibility to do it. You will not receive anything in return, and at the same time you will risk a great deal. But do it regardless, and don't feel that you are too good because of this. You are simply performing your duty. Act. Protect. In silence.

32

The Warrior Teaches

Someone has been waiting for you. A young apprentice has raised his prayers for his path to cross with yours. When you find him, stop. Do not commit the mistake of eluding your liability.

You will have to renounce your current lifestyle and dedicate time to your disciple. Devote yourself entirely to him. Be patient with his faults. Teach him in silence, help him to pacify his spirit, to take hold of his sword and to cut the chains.

He will bother you with a thousand and one useless and senseless questions. He will doubt you, and it is even possible that he will abandon you. But you must always be there with open arms to welcome him as your own son when he understands and returns.

You will be everything for him. His eyes will stare at you, eager for knowledge. He will observe your way of walking and will imitate it. He will copy the way you hold your fork because he

will foolishly think that this will bring him to illumination. But it does not matter. Some day he will understand.

When this moment arrives, you will have established one of the most beautiful relationships on this earth. You will be Master and Disciple. You will be one.

冨士三十六景
伊豆の山中

⟞⟝ 33 ⟞⟝

The Warrior Abandons Himself to the Almighty

Abandon yourself to destiny. Trust that everything will be for the better, even though you are not able to understand it now. Seat yourself. Breathe. Surrender.

There is nothing you can do now. Understand that you are only a man. A Warrior, but in the final instance a man. You have done everything possible. You have suffered what was necessary and even more. You have made the required effort. And even more. But it does not depend on you any longer. Neither retreat nor move forward, neither act nor remain still. Suspend yourself in the air, leaving everything in the hand of the Almighty.

34

The Warrior Erases his Track

Far away, the sun rises. It is the last time for me.
The wolves begin the journey.

Imagine that today is your last day. Are you ready to die? What things would be left hanging, unresolved with your death? What things would you regret not having done? Today is the day of erasing your traces. To tie up the loose ends, to close the circles, to sweep your footsteps. Say what you have to say, do what you have to do. May there be left only the Light of the Buddha in your roots, in your leaves.

Has it not been beautiful after all?

35

The Warrior Dies

You will surely miss the world, your loves, your battles. But do not grieve. You will come back.

The life of a Warrior is arduous. You are one thousand years old and it is long past the time to rest. Leave your weapons, sit beside your brother of the way. Side by side, gazing at the sunset in the silent desert.

36

The Warrior is Born

The snow has melted,
The forest breathes again.
The sun reflects over the pond ...
Once again.

❧ PICTURE CREDITS ❧

The images are listed below according to the section of the book or number of the reading with which they appear.

Introduction V&A Picture Library. *A Horseman Galloping* by Zeshin.

1 • The Bridgeman Art Library / Fitzwilliam Museum, University of Cambridge. *Fuji from Koshigaya Mushashi*, No. 14 in the series '36 Views of Mt. Fuji' by Utagawa Hiroshige.

2 • The Bridgeman Art Library / Private Collection. *Lake Kawaguchi at the Foot of the Fuji* by Eisho and Kikugawa Koitsu.

3 • The Bridgeman Art Library / Private Collection. *A Landscape and Seascape* from '60-Odd Famous Views of the Provinces' by Utagawa Hiroshige.

4 • V&A Picture Library. *Magnolia, an Eagle and the 'Toad' Wizard* by Utagawa Hiroshige.

5 • The Tokyo National Museum. *Views of the Tokaido Road* by Imamura Shiko.

6 • The Bridgeman Art Library / Private Collection. *The Ashikaga Fleet Sailing in to Attack Nitta* by Utagawa Kuniyoshi.

7 • The Bridgeman Art Library / Victoria & Albert Museum, London. *Carp* by Taito II.

8 • The Bridgeman Art Library / Fitzwilliam Museum, University of Cambridge. *Eagle over Susaki, Fukagawa*, No. 107 in the series 'Yedo Hyakkei' by Utagawa Hiroshige.

9 • V&A Picture Library. *Actor as the Priest Saigyohoshi* by Utagawa Kunimasa.

10 · The Bridgeman Art Library/British Library, London. *Rabbits and Grasses,* Kano School mid fifteenth century.

11 · ET Archive. *Japanese Samurai,* nineteenth century woodblock.

12 · The Bridgeman Art Library/British Museum, London. *Tanneijiro Grappling Under Water* by Kuniyoshi.

13 · Los Angeles County Museum of Art, Gift of Mr and Mrs Felix Juda. *Mt. Kashimayari from Mt. Happo, Japanese Alps,* 1932 by Ito Takashi.

14 · V&A Picture Library. *Warrior Monk Benkei and the Moon* by Yoshitoshi.

15 · The Bridgeman Art Library/Victoria & Albert Museum, London. *Nichiren Calming the Storm with an Invocation,* 1857 by Yoshimory.

16 · The Bridgeman Art Library/Private Collection. *Ships Returning to Harbour at Tempozan* by Yahimira Gakutei.

17 · The Bridgeman Art Library/British Museum, London. *Full Moon at Seba* from the series '69 Stations of the Kisokaido' by Utagawa Hiroshige.

18 · The Bridgeman Art Library/Private Collection. *Mountains and Coastline* from '36 Views of Mt. Fuji' by Utagawa Hiroshige.

19 · The Bridgeman Art Library/Christie's, London. *A Fisherman Standing on a Rocky Promontory at Kajikazawa in Kai Provence* from the series '36 Views of Mt. Fuji' by Katsushika Hokusai.

20 • The College Art Collection, Strang Print Room, University College London. *Drinking Sake Under a Maple Tree* by Gekko.

21 • Visual Arts Library/Artephot/Zauho Press. *Taishaku and Three Animals* by Kono Bairei.

22 • The Bridgeman Art Library/Victoria & Albert Museum, London. Lovers from *Poem of the Pillow* by Kitagawa Utamaro.

23 • Los Angeles County Museum of Art, Gift of Mr and Mrs Felix Juda. *Benten Shrine, Kakizaki, Shimoda, 1937* by Kawasi Hasui.

24 • The Bridgeman Art Library/Fitzwilliam Museum, University of Cambridge. *Fuji from Yuhi-Ga, Megwo*, No.10 in the series 'Fuji Saryu Rokkei' by Utagawa Hiroshige.

25 • The Bridgeman Art Library/Private Collection. *Portrait of Tokugawa Leyasu,* dictator from 1615–16, Japanese seventeenth century.

26 • The Bridgeman Art Library/Private Collection. *Retreat in the Mountains* by Tessai Tomioka.

27 • Los Angeles County Museum of Art, Gift of Mr and Mrs Felix Juda. *Tennoji (Temple) Osaka, 1927* by Kawase Hasui.

28 • V&A Picture Library. *Samurai and Warrior below Mount Fuji* by Okumura Toshinobu.

29 • Visual Arts Library/Private Collection. Untitled print by Hokusai.

30 • The Bridgeman Art Library/British Library, London. *Hisaka in the Sayo Mountains* by Utagawa Hiroshige.

31 · The Bridgeman Art Library/Private Collection. *Tokiwa-Gozen with her Three Children in the Snow* by Utagawa Kuniyoshi.

32 · V&A Picture Library. Drawing from a series entitled *Story of the Phantom Cat* by Kyosai.

33 · The Bridgeman Art Library/Fitzwilliam Museum, University of Cambridge. *Fuji from the Mountains of Isu,* No.22 from the series '36 views of Mt. Fuji' by Utagawa Hiroshige.

34 · The Bridgeman Art Library/Private Collection. *The Kintai Bridge in Springtime* by Hasui.

35 · San Diego Museum of Art, Gift of Mrs Clark M. Cavanee. *Above the Clouds* from the series 'Japan Southern Alps' by Yoshida Hiroshi.

36 · The Bridgeman Art Library/Fitzwilliam Museum, University of Cambridge. *Fuji from Koshigaya Mushashi,* No.14 in the series '36 Views of Mt. Fuji' by Utagawa Hiroshige.

❧ ACKNOWLEDGEMENTS ❧

Author's Acknowledgements

Many thanks go to my teacher and friend, 'Sir' Julian Whipple from Exeter High School, New Hampshire, USA. He helped me to create the English version of this book. For all his help and for what he has taught me, the first edition of this book is dedicated to him.

What you see, dear reader, results from the work of many people. To acquire True Vision, you must see the whole. Behind this book are Tessa Monina, Pritty Ramjee, Ian Jackson and Zoë Hughes, from Eddison Sadd Editions, with whom I am in debt.

Eddison • Sadd Editions

Editorial Director	*Ian Jackson*
Project Editors	*Zoë Hughes* & *Tessa Monina*
Proofreader	*Nikky Twyman*
Art Director	*Elaine Partington*
Art Editor	*Pritty Ramjee*
Calligrapher	*Koïchiro Fukasawa*
Picture Researcher	*Liz Eddison*
Production	*Karyn Claridge* & *Charles James*